At the beach

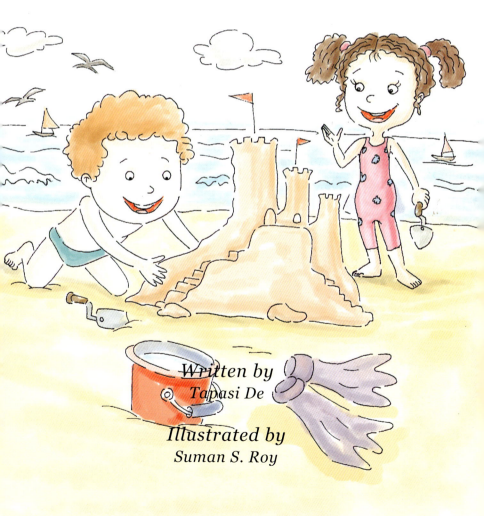

Written by
Tapasi De

Illustrated by
Suman S. Roy

It was a boring Sunday.

We were all home. We did not have anything to do.

We wanted to go out and enjoy our Sunday.

However, we had no idea where to go.

Just then, mum had an idea.

Mum said that we could go to the beach as it was sunny and warm.

We all thought it was a great idea!

We helped mum pack all the things we would need.

She made delicious sandwiches...

and packed different juices and sweets.

Dad packed our beach umbrella and a mat to spread on the sand.

We also took our swimsuits,

goggles, sun caps and sun protection lotion.

Mum packed all the food in a large picnic basket.

Finally, we were ready to go!

We all got into the car.
This time mum drove.

At the beach, the sea was blue and the sky was clear.

Dad planted the beach umbrella into the sand.

We spread out the mat under the umbrella and sat on it.

Mum took out the food for us to eat.

My sister and me ate the sandwiches and drank the juice. Mum and dad drank their tea.

We all changed into our swim suits quickly. My swim suit was green and my sister's was pink.

Then we started building a sand castle. We made a really big castle.

Meanwhile, mum and dad went for a swim. We could see them splashing in the water.

After the sand castle was made, we collected sea shells.

We then went for snorkelling.

There were colourful fishes, corals and different plants under the sea. It was a new world for us.

After a while, we came out of water. We were all tired but very happy.

We packed our things and got ready to go home.

When we reached home, it was evening. It was a wonderful Sunday!

Let's spell new words

enjoy

sunny

warm

idea

beach

packed

sandwiches

candies

swimsuit

goggles

lotion

protection

umbrella

picnic

basket

hour

building

collected

snorkelling

coral

wonderful